PRAISE FOR THE YEAR I LOVED ENGLAND

The Year I Loved England is rooted in place. The damaged terrain and the battered emotions become one, "a map of everything there's ever been" says *The Curve of Chaos*. This moving collection also offers some answers to its own complex, layered question, "Where is here anyway?", with answers that are both sensitive and vivid, in the voices of an England that it seems too many people have decided is too hard to love.
ANTHONY CARTWRIGHT (Author of *Heartland*)

Strong and moving and real. The Year I Loved England has a Jack Kerouac feel of beat beauty.
FRED VOSS

The objectives I wrote down whilst reading 'The Year I Loved England': evocative, poignant, surprising, funny, questioning and relevant… Great stuff.
HORACE PANTER (ska legend)

This poetry expresses poignantly the emotions that I at times find difficult to articulate. The words pierced my soul and brought back the images, emotions and feelings of those days in August 2011 when Britain burnt
TARIQ JAHAN

Horgan and Owen indict England for unforgivable failures both foreign and domestic while hinting at a country that might yet be. This is work marked by fury and frustration but also by a stubborn and beleaguered love.
BILLY RAMSELL

THE YEAR I LOVED ENGLAND

JOSEPH HORGAN & ANTONY OWEN

Photographs by Rangzeb Hussain

How come that they are out there, excluded from public space?
How come that you are in here, included in it?
Slavoj Žižek

Don't wanna be rich, don't wanna be famous.
The Specials

ADDRESS
After Marc Chagall

All the houses on our street are upside down
and people fly above the chimneys.
They are falling
in to the sky.

They are not from here anyway.
Not one of them is from here anyway.
Who is from here anyway?

The people in the sky are falling up,
in to India, Pakistan, Ghana, Nigeria,
St. Kitts and Ireland.
They are landing on their heads.

They are from here everyway.
Every one of them is from here someway.
Where is from here anyway?

All the streets near our house are downside up
and chimneys fly above the people.
They are sky
and they are flying.

SOMEWHERE

Art too is just a way of living….somewhere in a rugged reality

> Rainer Maria Rilke

There are lovers here.
Bearing flags of places they've left
they lay them down,
knowing colours say not
we belong
but,
you do not.

What do lovers care?
The silence of human hearts,
against which flags,
territories and states are merely
flutters in the breeze,
is where they live.

When evening comes
they turn the television on,
leave lights off,
put legs across,
touch hands in the glare,
close eyes,
their backs to the night.

GHOST TOWN

Once this gasping tunnel
stitched slate to bluebells
where navvies held fist fights.

A town was made by coal,
hills had their backs broken,
black mountains glimmered.

Men whinnied to the rest day
then chirruped like nightingales
in chapels of woodchip cold.

Dragonflies hung with jam jar newts,
their abdomens were sapphires
adorning mould furred walls.

Women floated from gramophones,
men ripped wildflowers from sleepers
to dance them to a life of bourbon.

The murdering wheel went still,
miners washed to pale men
hauling pauper's wood through a ghost town.

The bleak cargo wailed north
to a town of velveteen faces
and ports with Japanese flags.

COVENTRY STREET

This city lost another street today
a baker threw his thumbprints to birds,
legs of lamb were walked to a skip.

This street was named after a watchmaker,
his hands stroke the bell towers face
pigeons swoop for burgers there.

This city progressed today,
a busker buried his symphonies
walked headless to Starbucks.

My city lost its voice today,
in its stone grey throat
a song was soulless.

FLIGHTPATH

They think we see nothing.
I know what flight sounds like,
above blue slates
and the out-of-reach chimneys.
I have seen them going over,

the swirling flocks, the interminable
dance above subway or bus,
dance like the birth of a universe.
Don't worry, friend.
I have seen the world.

THE DREAMER OF SAMUEL VALE HOUSE

We sat by kerb trees denied of Autumn.
Watched the black and decker blossom that
brushed the eight fourteen to Courtaulds.

Tonight I'll tune into rain and blackbird aerials
make pictures from Air India clouds
watch magpies scrape song from tyre track birds.

With grade two bricks scrumped from the gatehouse
I'll watch bored kids re-open the factory
admire their work where there is none.

Tonight I'll walk you home to the sky
to floor thirty six we'll look down on everyone
and wish upon stars of a 747.

Everyone is leaving here or arrived from a tent,
I have googled the earth and am tired of paradise.
This city is home, I am its key and broken door.

CANDY CANE

The things they did at number twelve
were shrink wrapped in pallets
and sold in the flea market.

He pixelates womanhood,
downloading her pseudonym,
groping bodies with a cursor.

Dreams boil in baked spoons,
beaks of her arms opened,
slumped in alleyways of pierced veins.

Gannets of needles resurfaced,
from blue skin to spume,
wave after wave crashed a spent shell.

SLEEPLESS

Light out and light shines in.
A head light may strafe the room.
Movement breaks a stillness that makes
her bedroom.

She may watch the red digits change.
Clothes against a chair back the only
other ever here.
Light goes out and her day begins.

COMPLINE

In the end
this extra fat won't kill me.
Disorientation will do for me.

It's much more malignant.
This can be a dangerous place
if you stray off the beaten

path at the back of my house there are wild dogs.
They pass in and out of burnt cars
like polar bears on rubbish tips in Alaska.

I'll use a chain to beat them away.
I can make it to the tree cover.
Underneath a ribbon I'll wait for partisans.

If you read this after I'm gone.
The key is underneath the plant pot on the left.

THE YEAR I LOVED ENGLAND

A part of you was human in that rush hour
when brake-lights gouged their abscess of dead dreams.

I was asleep in the timed warmth of strike year,
factory kids were gaps in milk crates by classrooms.

In the years of your longest days I never went without a dad,
we only moaned as spitfires down keep out hills.

A part of me was adult when they broke you that Friday,
the down on your arms came from my pocket money.

In the year I loved England you plucked blackthorns from my hand,
rubbed away down from the nettle's sting.

In the year I loved England a man left the house
and returned unmade from the smokeless factory.

In the year I loved England my dad lost his dad,
found an orphan grey in the glass.

I was awake when you should have been sleeping,
you timed your grief into your father's shirt.

There is a poem stuffed in sad black suits,
for father's we bury and resurrect,
from clothes that wear us with yesterday's sweat.

COVENTRATE

There are snowflakes on a charred cross,
a replica in your retina,
the true stained windows of new Cov.

The mowed down tulips on Gibbet Hill
grew from wheels of coaled black hair
trimmed off men who coughed in barber shops.

There's a man strapping spikes above Greggs,
pigeons roost in echo dead factories
where men migrated to the job centre.

The moved on skateboarder spills out his pants,
always on his arse since the signs came,
he's bloody useless everyone says.

There are flowers hung from lampposts on Radford Road,
a girl mowed down by a raghead in a 30,
they're fucking everywhere the patriots say.

There were black boys plucking snowballs from their hair,
white boys washing coal from their face,
an albino crow hatching from Cofa's Tree.

Coventry derived from the Saxon name Cofa's Tree

FAT MAN

"You ask what is our aim? I can answer in one word. It is victory. Victory at all costs. Victory in spite of all terrors. Victory however long and hard the road may be, for without victory there is no survival"

                                        Winston Churchill, May 13th, 1940

Oh ribbon weaver
what did you weave in the war room
for Coventry?

Fine sky blue yarns,
fat Havana halos, the prophetic ligature
for stained black saints.

Oh war shepherd
the mauling wolves embed our moon,
torn against our spire.

Toe tags queue for names,
a child they thought was a beam
was younger than your brandy.

Oh ribbon weaver
what will you weave for Dresden
from Coventry's stone elbows?

The Nagasaki bastard
they named after you
whistled like a soldier,

bloomed for the lotus flower,
your carbonised legacy.
Fat Man, fire, criminal.

PLACE

I can be found at number seven A.
I have placed myself here,
have a living
and somewhere you can send to me
all of the things
I cannot see.
Do not forget and send soon.
I long to read and remember.
Be assured,
I still have hope.
Between my teeth.
Yes, I still have hope, truly,
between
my
teeth.

METROPOLIS

These are my constellations,
windows of no-go tower blocks,
my personal Orion without the myth.

Our days and nights are wound
by cogs of gold and silver,
my alarm is *Petrov* leaving for work.

I can flick a star through a switch,
be a part of the uptown universe,
shoot across hills on my moped

to the black hole where worlds queue to end,
sucked into the dark matter
of form after form.

SEXT

I should eat more fruit.
Cut down on the gin.
Use a bicycle in the bedroom.

My mind creaks,
my body is becoming unhinged.
An old door in a fence.

Health, you see, is a passing enchantment,
an illusion of the years.
The ultimate con trick.

Not that I'm unwell, you understand,
it's just that this is an old
house where things take place.

When I sleep in the day.
I feel as if the dead are singing.

THE LITTLE THINGS DESTROY US

When I was a son
you closed with the factories,
broke things to fix them.

You grew a moustache,
wore unemployed clothes,
caged your world in a shed.

That black leg Easter you wept,
Thatcher glided in a Daimler,
like spit on union coats.

In the blue asbestos sleet
you groaned with embroidered steel,
hocking slush in shiny basins.

The Christmas Nissan cancelled
you wrapped the road in fumes,
tore through sleet with a grimace.

I was your son a long time ago,
when I raced to the gate
of your Kawasaki symphony.

Childhood was an itchy caravan
on a site full of white folk
wrestling with wind breakers.

Childhood was a magic trick,
it vanished with the work,
sometime in the eighties.

That day I ran into blackthorns
you plucked them out like feathers,
the plume of your pipe calmed me.

The little things destroy us,
anchors to childhood are heavy,
sometimes they drown us.

TERCE

I ring work and tell them.
I am not coming in today.
In case this is the day I die

I explain that I don't want
my last day on earth
to be spent in there.

I am malfunctioned,
should be returned,
to the warehouse.

I am on the end of the bed.
Heavy rain striates the glass.
Sounds like brick falling.

If the phone rings, you know.
It isn't me.

PADDIES

And all around here there were Paddies,
on this street and that street, down there,
Paddies, and they had their social clubs here,
and there, look, there, they had their church
and the school where their kids went,
loads and loads of kids,
running around the place with their Paddy
names and their Paddy faces

and their English accents,
Paddies all over the place around here,
though their kids were more or less invisible,
disappearing Paddy kids and you hardly saw
their women except for picking up the kids
or doing some shopping, coming out of mass,
it was the Paddies, see, Paddies everywhere,
Paddies everywhere around here,
putting it all together, raising it up,
Paddies who'd hardly seen a tarmacked road,
come out of this wet field and that,
to furnish a city, Paddies, Paddies,
Paddies everywhere around here.

BOOTHS

They scaled glaciers of salt,
raised clouds and sick children,
built a new way of life and death.

We skipped in fatherless cul-de-sacs,
sailed paper yachts down Kitchener Street,
raced pooh sticks in the slurry.

We hopscotched to adulthood,
Mrs Murphy's eyes burnt mass,
washing away the chalk of our communion.

They towed her son with a borrowed nag,
the lungs rosary confessed on heather,
secrets of salt alpines.

Look east to multiplex mountain,
where Saint Mary's was condemned,
people still struggling to change in booths.

FOUR O'CLOCK

This lad is staring through the window
watching his father's grizzled dreams;
the motor up on bricks
he got off Donaghy across the way.

His mother reads Take a Break
in a bath on the side of the house;
lowering herself in to the water,
authentic life in her hands.

The weather is turning,
bitumen, concrete and brick grow cold;
a window frame rattles and shakes
the shot of graffiti smut on a wall.

The Jamaican man stops
and two men talk into the engine;
Dragon stout and Jameson's whiskey
warm the worn upholstery of dreams.

Four o'clock in the afternoon.
Goalposts are ghost white in the park.
Lights come on in the rows of street.
This lad feels the freezing dark surround him.

AFTER THE ACCIDENT

What part of a car are you?

Some people think
they are the engine.

Some people think
they are the bull bar,
impaling the bird.

Some people think
they are the tyres,
that will never blow.

I think I'm the mirrors,
looking back.

DISADVANTAGED AREA

There are twenty one fruits at Jaspal's
weighed by hands of henna and lace.
The old woman never says thank you.
Her father sleeps in the biggest room.
There are three generations at Jaspal's.

There were two men from uptown fighting.
Vote red for change blue for change.
The disadvantaged area is our priority.
There were fourteen spices in the air.
Sikhs buying fruit from Hindus.

If you want a macchiato take a bus uptown,
past church, gurdwara, mosque and park,
get off by the nursing home at Costa;
there are three of them to choose from where Gaz
got jumped for his IPAD.

THE SUBJECTS

Machines gleamed in the fifties.
Cobbled streets were chrome and ruin;
sky basked in bonnets of Daimler.

Men were produced by factories.
On Sundays air smelt of *Dreft*,
only wives hung out husbands to dry.

Coal crackled fire in miner's chests,
the breathing city was spat in to cups,
ruins emerged from ruins.

People walked with their heads up.
Moon awaited America,
like Guinness for the Irish to settle.

Slab grey streets flowed rivers of Sari,
they made their gold in street corners,
sweeping crystals of shop windows,

these anagrams of broken English
made Urdu a backroom language
where fathers drifted home through incense.

Children played on stairwells to sun,
shooting down immigrant planes
from houses that would die again.

These were my father's streets.
He forged silver from mackerel,
walked through welded rain.

These were my grandma's streets.
The one who gave me cake and coin,
to buy bread from the nig-nog.

These were my mother's streets.
the one who pushed a glass eye pram,
to men with war in their eyes.

This city bore its country's scar.
Healed by all of its subjects,
our city invaded all of us.

THE SHELF STACKER

On riot black bricks
a welder sprayed the lie
washed away by unnoticed youths
doing their time in high vis.

Sunset is chained to a swing,
its mural bled in the playground
with fists of a jobseeker,
searching the works of rage.

Our streets gleam gold in the rain,
derelict shops are cold beds of youth
clutching their stomachs,
like cheap handbags.

Downtown the streets are cleaned for trade,
diamonds of a cobbler's window brushed into bags,
a youth wears his preacher's label,
the welder forced to stack shelves.

STATE FUNERAL

In a hundred unseen ways.
In the leaf mould beneath trees
as winter steps in.
At the back of a car
as frost fades.
In the hallway,
half-way to the door.
Beneath the flyover
as taillights flee.

By a bare path on the island.
In the back of a Glasgow flat.
Under the baking Kashmiri sun.
On the boat that never arrives.

In a hundred unseen ways.

FAUN

Here come the sons of Adam,
half-human fauns conjoined,
bones of a bagpipe's lament.

Here come the father's of war,
heads bowed with bucket flowers,
amputated like benefits.

Here come three lions roaring on cloth,
laid to rest on a stone table,
squeaking on rope over Whitehall Narnia.

Here come the true flags,
furred clothes wearing wardrobes,
the last battle *lost*.

Here come the real hymns for God,
a lifetime of two minute silences,
bugles turning fauns to stone.

LOGO

In the twice murdered park
they cordoned off frost,
diggers stabbed the paddling pool.

In hypodermic dew
tarmac clung to a see-saw,
a robin bloodied the bough.

Come April where blossom used to fall,
we'll drink cappuccino, get caught in moments
like carrier bags on bus level trees.

Come April we can queue outside Primark,
I'll buy me a new me
on the playground I discovered myself.

Come March I shall walk to the swings,
push the seat where fathers made childhoods
and gob the way Darren did.

Come March I'll peel paint from the carousel,
reveal the name of a lay student
who necked wine and a teachers tongue.

Come March sky is a logo.

ZOOLOGY

You can sail from Dudley to Africa
through pools of a primate's eyes,
leave splash marks in the iris,
slice cheeks of apples
from fenced off trees.

You can lay with leopards in grey savannahs,
stroke stripes of an iron ribcage,
watch gazelle crawl from carrier bags
and meat lap away ghosts
frowning from the water.

You can watch Pandas in foie-gras love hives,
chow bamboo from *Dobbie's World*
as the world gets it on.
These animals are toys
stuffed with manmade threads.

COLD STORAGE

I have journeyed Hull through Venetian blinds,
felt Louisiana jazz sieved through elevators,
smelt fields of sprayed lavender on floor nineteen.
I am filed in Milton Keynes under miscellaneous.

I have poured voyages of ships through crucibles,
watched moon roll clams for gulls and migrants,
saved my whole life for a whole life with Niamh.
I poured her in the sea en-route to Wexford.

I am flashing before you on a memory stick,
our lives are briefly connected and then.
We shut down in the machine.

THE HOUSE WITH ITS LIGHTS OFF

We double bagged their decades,
a chipped ballerina from Benidorm,
the blushing bride in black and white,
her red garter tied to love letters,
this starved room is ready now.

In a box marked bric and brac
doilies floated like dirty snowflakes,
the ones she spent a month of Sundays
cross stitching silk over errors
used from odds and sods.

There is a photograph older than us,
the one she hid in a *Mills and Boon,*
they were younger than all of us,
he was feeding her strawberries,
rain washed the plates.

OTHER PLACES

We don't just live in this house.
Rain still curves our spines.
Sun still fences us beneath a tree.
We miss our footing by the river
and effluent washes skin away.
There are fish with diseased heads.
We turn the lid upside down when we have drunk tea.
Then we freewheel all the way to town.
In the picture house we get our invites
and are seduced.
We don't go to graveyards after the first time.
If we go at all.
Rain still lands when we sleep.
Sun still wakes us.
We live in all the other places too.

SEASON TICKET

There is movement in the film
and a pub above railway sidings,
or a junction
with the city laid out;
country of mast and track,
undiscovered miles and lives,
bread and power strikes
bringing candles and laughter.
This is the street too.

Or it is evening
and floodlights sing a congregation,
swaying, smoking, swearing,
old industrial identities,
and ninety minutes can be long
but forgetting is longer;
a copper lifting over
into sixty thousand people.
Have you ever heard that song?

An immigrant father picks his way
through terraced ranks of identity
and a riot against people just the same
is a morality play in streetlights;
police light the backdrop to guilt,
is the street I remember
and longed to get so far away
to find the longing to go back.
Really, this is the street too.

THE CURVE OF CHAOS

My heart is pounding.
I am the curve of this street,
gambolling from door to door,
a map of everything
there's ever been.
Something gambols in my chest.
I am a map of gathering,
on a street of gambols I am.
The lucky curving man.

My heart is tired.
At the age I am
I'm lucky to gather
another curve of the universe
into my lungs.
I'm lucky the electricity is still on.
The curve of chaos;
I'm lucky the age I am.
Lucky as electricity.

My tired heart
is running down this street.
Lucky electric lungs
curving in a gambol.
I'm lucky to live
on the curved gathering of chaos.
Electric gambols in my chest
and running down it is.
My lucky pounding heart.

PRIME

The buzz of an alarm and footfalls.
Bed creak through the wall
and a body shifting.

The working day.
I hear smothered voices
as of someone trying to reach me.

But I don't think they are.
I hear a cat
screaming in my head.

This wall is a breeze
block through the gaps and clearings,
I hear lives.

They don't know any of this of course.
I'm telling you first.

VERMIN

A fox came to Powell Estate,
sipped sky from my bird-table.
We exchanged territories.

Ablaze in mist she glided to leftovers.
Cities have eaten the forest,
her snout sews the green man's ghost.

Vermin and baby made front pages.
I read in a side column not long ago
they were shooting dogs in Rwanda.

AFTER THE MASTIFF

All it took was whites removed from colours,
wind ripping her arms from the line,
a dog barking at a dog barking.

All it took was her daughter dancing from pegs,
ballet shoes wound a music box of rain,
one last dance dripped from tiptoes.

All it took were bouquets stuffed through railings,
the chill of a sunflower's flame,
burnt offerings, embers of a calyx.

All it took was a latch from another world,
the cowering cloth scrunched in a ball,
dog and daughter tied from Mother's cord.

TECHNOLOGICAL UNIVERSE

I am out
in the atomic facts of the world
but blind to it all
move like flickering light,
like a fox at night,
I am the wonder
of a technological universe,
out,
in the bare facts of the world,
gulping cold air
lying down,
in my own backyard.

FITTING IN

Ash shortened his name to fit in,
grouted slabs with Marlboro red,
quaffed tokes with part-time skinheads.

Ash told jokes, the one about a Hindu
forcing Gandhi to smoke from the chest,
the gun's turban daubed three bindis.

Ash became Ashraf on Fridays,
never fit in at the mosque,
wore Levi Strauss and unwashed feet.

A joke went round on the common,
that Ash prayed west in a skinhead's shadow
shortening his life to fit in.

BEFORE THE RAIN CAME

Our ring road is a forced marriage
of IKEA sky once held together
by medieval beams.

Many times my city has walked through me
and turned to stone in my eyes
when I took a piss on Spon Street.

A pub served mead the old way here,
landlords made way for baristas
boasting fair-trade on tax free plots.

Our city was made by flames,
the phoenix was a welder's torch,
men like my Da before the rain came.

Our city was a blank canvas
two tones barely mixing,
bleeding separately away from each other.

Many times my brothers walked past me
down Foleshill Road in the rain,
those colours should have ran.

Then Coventry would be grey,
two tone,
beautiful.

RATTLES AND SHAKES

The things they put through the letterbox.
Little knowing that I was sitting out the back.
Always out the back.
A watchful dog

on the doorstep, alive, alert.
In my plain yard of dirt.
Every slab removed,

my work is done.
To the letterbox they can come.
I am waiting for the sun.

THE BURNING OF NUMBER EIGHT'S WHEELIE BIN

Maybe it was that Tuesday, her yapping handbag,
a faux leather finger stiff to the natives.

The Waitrose van on a dropped kerb driveway
where offending leylandii blocked patriotic tenements.

Maybe it was that Friday when Iqbal knocked her door
with rainbows of Lahore in tin foil cartons,

showed off his Audi, took her for a spin,
where windows change to plywood at the mosque.

Boys in makeshift burkas sprayed white nigga with a typo,
they ran with paint staining the streets.

Last Tuesday the ginnell shone gold from her wheelie bin.
They found bones of lamb dopiaza and a Pekinese.

NATIVES

Our omens came through bugs
drumming your windshield,
dying as art with a rear view star,
glimmering with road kill.

Cats' eyes glowered on lover's lane,
the sluice of rain and rushed intercourse,
thawed your innards of emptiness,
a fuck warm smog tried to escape us.

Clouds rolled with rizla on breastbone,
you wished upon a marijuana moon
and in the starlit sarcophagus
you showed your true face.

On a long drive you learn things,
foxes stay still for tyres,
their twitching kaleidoscopes
leave truths in black and white.

We are all native in moonlight, she said,
like dusk we haemorrhage to bone,
scattered archives of dulled eyes
in split second journeys of ice.

VANISH

Let's vanish.
Right now, upstairs,
five o'clock in the day,
when we should be coming
home from work
or walking back from the shop,
a conspiracy of two,
right now, at the front door,
two fingers to a world
that isn't watching,
even listening
to sirens in the street,
no harm
in arms and whispers,
right now.
Let's vanish.

THE STUDENT WHO PISSED ON A WAR MEMORIAL

That night you must have pulled moon there,
watched it float with names of stale heroes
through a yellow fog of *Jagermeister.*

You must have noticed those plastic wreaths
weep from stone where suits ate bagels
and freshmen upload laughs to feel connected.

You must have noticed the wooden cross
left for men necking rum for a yard;
some wet from whistle blowers.

Their fog was a devil's dress
a khaki sea of claimed islands,
eyes pulled back by two full moons.

I never noticed your apology,
scantily clad like binge drinkers
collapsing with new widows.

THEY COULD PAPER THE MOON

I'm not ashamed of my small triumphs.
Not that I warrant a trumpet or a song,
I'll dance everyday anyway and have no need
of those who have so much money
they could paper the moon.
I have no need and they have so many.

When summer comes I sit on the doorstep.
Nothing gives me more life than watching
lovers fight and doors get slammed
or someone stands in the street and yells, I wonder,
where they are now and if they are still in love
or fight with someone else.

ALL THEIR BRICK WALKS

They think I am
about buses and flyovers,
as if I a man,
with a field inside his head,
a squall of rain beating
against the panes of his skull,
carries a grá for all their brick,
walks their enduring shelters,
their seductive corner lighting,
with anything but eyes
in the back of my head
and the runt of a thorn tree
curving itself to the shape
of a wind.

DEAD AIR

Their silence
is a radio play
and they are
a song
amongst interruption.
There is nothing above this.
She says nothing.
He says nothing.
Sweet loveliness of nothing.
She leans across.
He leans across.
Some songs, see,
only belong in the air.

THE YOUNG SOLDIER'S FUNERAL

At the catalogued sermon
old psalms staggered with a squaddie's fiancé
draped in new life.

Enthusiastic organist
shrilled with loose change
in brushed suede begging bowls.

Her astro-turf lover lowered
where heroes are born
to eight foot darkness

Pinned to a cellophane bouquet
a hallmark verse clung to a cliché
of a choked full stop.

Tonight she drowned in Eminem
to surface in something familiar,
his face aglow in the alkaline hearth.

SOIL FEE

Raw meat hung from taxi ranks
hailing night's metered hearses,
two for one sick, jet-washed away.

Rashmi picked up a fare,
two lovers going all the way
he wiped away their clouds,

sprayed moonlight from a pothole,
thought of Mumbai slums
and skins of monsoon gold.

He warned the lovers of the soil fee,
they morphed to spray tanned racists.
'*Whatever coon*,' she said.

UNBRANDED
For Tariq Jahan

On looting flames
a thousand heads were snowdrops;
six slippers queued for three dead sons.

This is our blooding,
the corpse of red sky dragged to a new dawn
where shops are foxholes.

Politicians ride purring horses to middle England
to find it was never there on their watch.
The kennelled youth whimper for attention

barking like Chihuahuas to bulldogs,
feeding pilau rice into cameras
and Terry's chocolate orange into Ugg boots.

An orphaned father asks for calm,
his son's young face flushed with freckled blood,
covered in unbranded cotton.

He could have stolen a moment
to read his eyes as rioters ignored bookshops,
groping Reebok from anorexic mannequins.

The old fountain never let his face go,
wrinkling him only once to be ancient,
cleansing his cheap tossed wishes of youth.

In the amniotic zip bag
he sailed linoleum
to his mother moored in grief.

His face once glowed like Debenhams,
a kindling of skin cold in siren blue,
waiting for paradise.

MONK AND MARGINALIA

They put it in the margins.
Exactness. Bird's eye view.
A blackbird sings
for a thousand years.

We could stay here.
If we were true. Honest to a fault.
Run up the darkened street
for a hundred years.

So to be the aside.
Off centre. Shine a light.
Our brick house stands
for a million years.

CONCEALMENT

In the city too
watching things themselves
is to repair our broken knowledge.

At the bus stop a kestrel
scatters sparrows
and there is sky above traffic.

To this place of reluctance
departing birds come.
A fox steals from a bin.

There is a shore of broken glass
beneath the swings.
We live
in the space between the buildings.

I THINK OF ALL THE MOONS I HAVE SEEN
'The extremists are afraid of books and pens.'
Malala Yousafzai

I am a girl,
a sixteen year old girl

and one day I will be a woman,
I will be a woman,

so I spit pomegranate seeds,
I spit pomegranate seeds,

though I have lived
my whole life in this city,

sixteen years in this city,
my whole life

and I turn to the window
and make a recording

in an older way,
turn to the window

and see my own face,
my sixteen years,

and rain hits the window,
rat-atat-tat,

like rain hitting the window,
rat-atat-tat,

and my face is smiling,
my whole face.

And my beautiful life.

I THINK MY PARENTS MADE LOVE

I carry my children to dreams,
it's there I rest in the dusk of eyelids,
whispering your name into waves,
trying to write it before they break.

I carry my child in the pit of my stomach,
each school run dawn yawning with Mothers,
the odd boy tightropes kerbs to miss cracks.
I think he was made and named in a rush.

Whilst asleep my inner child awakens me,
I call out to chemical echoes
the names that named me at birth,
my life becomes the translation.

My Mother used to lift me in to the sky,
I took my first steps on the stars,
fell over as a man where the odd boy walks.
When I was made, I think my parents made love.

LITTLE CEREMONIES

Come to post war landfill,
open mouths are strummed by orderlies
like horsehair on woodwind.

Sip their sour ingested calmness,
watch Nosferatu shadows
wail soundproofed hauntings.

Listen to the father's small talk,
the price of fags and unlikely regards
of a bedwetting brother.

Walk to the spray can lake
where bloated swans make burials beautiful
from broken arms of bread.

These little ceremonies of war
forget the world around them
as we do theirs, building our mail order nests.

STREETLIGHTS

The things that happen in houses
sometimes happen to us.

Walls and doors
to keep ourselves in
and lock ourselves out.

Streetlights on and everyone
takes to the doorstep.
Lights a candle. Clicks a lighter.

Sets fire to the bin.

All night long
the houses
are dark and empty.

VISITORS

I bleached your room for a newcomer,
exhumed the cotton archaeologies,

your porcelain face to a bone china sky,
my eyes a chalice of spilt life.

Last Sunday after bingo and ovaltine,
snails shattered our footsteps,

a grandson killed you twice
with savage questions from the tender place.

The visitor moved in last October,
you raked in leaves with clumps of hair.

The dusk of your left breast shone
through nylon and calomine,

that night you slept with Paddy Quinn,
the *Liffey* pulled you home through his lilt.

DUSK ON HARROW HILL

The song sheet pylons throb,
chords of ice and sea salt skin
plucked like dragged lip lovers.

Dusk is a harsh desert;
birds rip varicose rivers,
gullets pulse for dead fish.

A girl disappeared last June,
skipping to a silhouette,
pounding earth with a gosling.

They're burning gorse to look for her,
the covered man points down,
hardened men are vomiting.

NONES

This house is winter.
My steps July tracks in the snow,
my breath cloud at the window.

Beneath acid trees;
limbs beneath soil.
A map of aged roots.

Partisans leave bright ribbons
as markers showing the way.
Colour silent in the day.

In the memory of this street
lies the way through.
Of all who passed by.

I could find my front door in the longest night.
As if I had been here forever.

THE STREET A POET MIGHT HAVE LIVED ON

> I was lifted up
> past rotten bricks weeds
> to look over the wall
>   Thomas Kinsella

There's something outside number one hundred.
The disco dance of an ambulance
and someone running to the phone.
There's a dog trapped in a shed.

On the street nothing happens for a long time.
Then a family is gone as if invisible
people could vanish.
And what happened

to those intimate strangers?
From a place where arteries harden,
a street where children skip
school as children in a meadow skip,

a street that is a meadow,
singing past hardened arteries.
Weeds and rotten brick
coming away in the hand.

A place to find the unlikely heart
of everyone who began elsewhere and knows.
There's no achievement
in knowing where you're from.

THREE FILMS ABOUT SILENCE

FLAT (1)

We need fresh horses.
I am looking through a window
and you sit
on the empty sofa.
Here we are
enacting all the rituals.
I should say,
get up honey, tables of dissolution wait
and after
we get a cross-country bus
because it isn't true
there is no there,
there is only here,
it isn't true,
and you say,
but how,
how do we
get to the rest of the world
from here?
But that might sully the art.
Summer evening.
You stay there.
I'll go back to the window.
Summon up fresh horses.
You sit on the empty sofa.

JOB APPLICATION (2)

And I would like, at least once,
to drink whiskey for breakfast,
like the wedding day and doorway
of the conquering terraced house;
drink it first thing with ghosts,
or the time on the train
passing it backwards and forwards
in front of the ticket holders.
I would like to have that breath.

And I would walk up to the ticket conductor,
see the wanting in his eyes,
the red brake of his dreams,
say stop the train now, compadre,
it's the end of the line
for you and I
and take his hand and jump,
the two of us rolling down the sidings,
past the swollen orange coats,
running down the line,
neat whiskey athletes.
The final shot.

ENDREEL (3)

The best silence
is in the gaps.
In the empty inner-city house,
in the lull between engines,
in the tap room as it opens
and the ferocious adherents
of the suburbs
depart.

From the doorstep,
pan over the streets
as far as St. Alphonsus Church,
over the roofs
of houses and of cars.
This is silence.
Here run the credits,
no one ever reads.

Acknowledgements

Poems have previously appeared in The Stinging Fly, The Echo Room, The Meadowland Review (USA), The International Hiroshima Peace Museum, The Wilfred Owen Story, The Stony Thursday Book, Poetry Nottingham International, Abridged, The Lake, Turbulence, Ink Sweat & Tears, Alliterati, Snorkel (Australia), Stepaway Magazine, Weary Blues (New Binary Press) Brick Rhetoric (USA), Ancient Heart (Australia), Kumquat, Nous, Boscombe Revolution, Message In A Bottle, Ten Years in The Doghouse Anthology, Restless Bones: An Anthology for The Born Free Foundation.

Joseph Horgan was born in Birmingham, England, of Irish parents. He is a poet, author, journalist, and reviewer. His writings and poems have appeared in numerous literary journals in Ireland, the UK, Europe and America and have been broadcast on television and radio.

A past winner of The Patrick Kavanagh Award he has been shortlisted for a Hennessy Award and was chosen for the Poetry Ireland Introduction Series. He has received an Irish Arts Council bursary and a Cork County Council Arts bursary.

He has been a visiting writer at the Irish Writers in London Summer School and writer in residence at the Heinrich Boll cottage on Achill Island.

His first collection of poetry, Slipping Letters Beneath the Sea, was published by Doghouse in 2008. His second book, The Song at Your Backdoor, a meditation on identity and place, was published by Collins Press in 2010. It was selected as an RTE Book on One. His third book, An Unscheduled Life, a collaboration with the artist Brian Whelan, was published by Agenda Editions in 2012. His CD of poetry and traditional music *Men Without Names*, funded by County Cork Arts Department will be released in 2014.

His work has been anthologised in Off the Wall (Marino ed Niall MacMonagle), Landing Places (Dedalus ed Eva Bourke and Borbala Farago), and in the 2008-2011 Sunday Miscellany anthology. His journalism has appeared in Ireland and the UK, in the Irish Left Review, the Press Gazette and the Irish Post. He has written a weekly column for the Irish Post since 1999.

'A singular voice in Irish poetry' —Paula Meehan.

Antony Owen is from Coventry, England. His first collection *My Father's Eyes Were Blue* was published by The Heaventree Press in 2009. In 2011 Pighog selected Owen's manuscript *The Dreaded Boy* to launch the 'Passport' pamphlet series.

Poems from *The Dreaded Boy* were filmed and featured in 2012 by Staffordshire Poet Laureate Mal Dewhirst for an officially authorised and updated musical dramatisation of *The Wall* by *Pink Floyd*. *The Wilfred Owen Story & Port Sunlight Museum* selected his poem The Stinging as a 2011 competition finalist. In 2010 *The Shine Journal* USA awarded his poem *Sangin* a runner up for their 2010 poetry competition.

In 2011 Owen was selected alongside Joel Lane by Amnesty International UK and Jacqui Rowe (Flarestack Press) to represent them for their 50th Anniversary centenary event. In 2013 Owen had an exhibition of poetry and photography accepted by the curator of the Hiroshima Peace Museum. This exhibition also featured in 2012 at Coventry Cathedral.

In association with Paul Casey, (*O'Bheal, Cork*), Owen volunteers his time as twin city coordinator for Coventry which sees an annual reciprocal exchange of poets each year from both cities. As part of this exchange Owen has travelled throughout Ireland with O'Bheal which included readings at many festivals including a reading at The Seamus Heaney Centre at Queens University, Belfast.

'Owen is only one of a handful of younger poets unafraid to write for these violent times. This is an uncompromising and timely poetic intervention, one that consolidates a serious talent.' Billy Ramsell

The year I loved England

© 2014 Joseph Horgan, Antony Owen and Pighog Publishing Ltd

Joseph Horgan and Antony Owen have asserted their right to be identified as the authors of this work in accordance with the Copyright, Designs and Patents Act 1998.

All rights reserved. No part of this pamphlet may be reproduced, stored in a retrieval system, or transmitted in any form, or by any means, electronic or otherwise, without the prior written permission of Pighog.

This publication is sold subject to the condition that it shall not, by way of trade or otherwise, be lent, resold, hired out or otherwise circulated without the publisher's prior consent in any form of binding or cover other than that in which it is published and without a similar condition including this condition being imposed on any subsequent purchaser.

A CIP record for this publication is available from the British Library.

Design by Jackson Rees

ISBN 978-1-906309-42-8

First published July 2014 by

Pighog
PO Box 145
Brighton BN1 6YU
England UK

info@pighog.co.uk
www.pighog.co.uk
Twitter: @pighog
Facebook: Pighog
Pinterest: Pighog